Sequel

poems by

Wendell Hawken

Finishing Line Press
Georgetown, Kentucky

Sequel

Copyright © 2019 by Wendell Hawken
ISBN 978-1-63534-966-5 First Edition
All rights reserved under International and Pan-American Copyright Conventions. No part of this book may be reproduced in any manner whatsoever without written permission from the publisher, except in the case of brief quotations embodied in critical articles and reviews.

ACKNOWLEDGMENTS

"Hawk" and "Are Sunsets More Beautiful in Winter?" appeared in *Clarke's Great Outdoors: A collection of artwork, poems, essays and photographs inspired by nature in Clarke County, VA* (The Piedmont Environmental Council, 2018).

Deep thanks to Dinah Berland, David Ruekberg, Susan Sindall, and Mary-Sherman Willis, all members of the Wally tribe, for their generous attention and thoughtful critiques of earlier drafts of this manuscript.

Publisher: Leah Maines
Editor: Christen Kincaid
Cover Art: Trisha Adams, *Winter Sunshine* oil on canvas
Author Photo: Matthew Klein
Cover Design: Elizabeth Maines McCleavy

Printed in the USA on acid-free paper.
Order online: www.finishinglinepress.com
               also available on amazon.com

                    Author inquiries and mail orders:
                          Finishing Line Press
                              P. O. Box 1626
                        Georgetown, Kentucky 40324
                                 U. S. A.

Table of Contents

Hawk 1

The Ruby-Throats Remember their Flowers 2

At Six O'Clock 3

Mute Light 4

When Ever 5

Cow Path 6

Spousal Psalm in the Key of C Major 7

Annus Mirabilis, Annus Horribilis at the Rock's Hard Place 8

Swallow 14

Due to the Attraction of the Moon and Sun 15

Before My Lover Was a Bird 16

Rock the Billy Goat Out of his Gruff 17

Are Sunsets More Beautiful in Winter? 18

On Re-Reading the Hospice Journal 19

Small Dark Mysteries 22

Aubade at Kitchen Window 23

Hawk

Lowbrow clouds of cotton candy
unspun across the sky—

the day's pink start
amplifies the hum of Interstate 81,

the vague rumble of freight steel on steel,
cross-track bleat of air horns.

If you could walk the lane with me,
the dogs and me, you would see yourself

how the fescue's green turns caramel,
the white glaze night frost lays on pasture,

a sight he would call *new snow*.
Can almost hear him say it: *new snow*.

It's not that I disdain your concrete,
your rise of soldered steel, the jostling.

I know its jolt and drive,
remember neon's night excitements,

the high heel beat on pavement—
did I really walk that way?—

but here, twice now, a female red-tail
sat perched on the fence, not ten feet away

unmoving as I drove down the lane—
eye to fierce unflinching eye.

The Ruby-Throats Remember Their Flowers, How Long Each Takes to Refill

We might learn to love
in hummingbird

each to the other's blossoms
deep and sweet

extracting one
from the other's need

alternating bird to blossom,
blossom, bird—here, now here

into each sweet crease
of beloved cover

where murmured words
turn bird:

beige burnished thoughts
best expressed in sparrow,

lark, and wren to leave
awe's stark and skyward

message to the blue-black
flap of crows.

At Six O'Clock

The sound he makes
when I set his dinner down:

his lips go soft,
open as a mollusk opens:

the same wet welcome
when I would stretch to meet

him where he stood,
eyes half-closed, head tilted down

in the days when
I was food.

Mute Light

Wrapped in a dark cloak
cloaking sight, the ears
hear rodents rustle moonstruck.

A struck-numb sun lifts
drifts of dark cloth as the farmer
farms grass pasture, plowing silt
built by swollen overflow.

How the river gifts the downstream
slipstream against a backstroke oar.

Hear the white words mumble until
chilled limbs grow numb
from cold-burn ever closer,
closer to the time all become
numb-struck under withdrawn sun.

When Ever

When ever
rolls over
and closes its eye,
the *e* of its eye

the vision of *e*
and wanders for ever
as over
will flow

its sense to the sea,
the roundness of *o*
for ever and ever
as over will go.

But never forever—
remember:
if ever it's over,
leave her.
Come home.

Cow Path

Sunset, the cows came in the yard. To them
an open gate is irresistible. I walked them back

the way they came. They like to go the way they come,
content with going where they've been, easy walking

where it's worn away, head to tail repeating earlier meanders.
Sunset, the west-facing three board fence glowed

pinkish-peach—that intense, the sky. The grass smelled fresh cut,
so uniform to be not grass but a smooth green fabric.

Two bay horses side by side in the back paddock
far enough away to be not actual, but ideas.

A matched pair. Or of a like mind. Heads down,
grazing their own growing shadows, just two quiet concepts

in a confinement of parallel pink lines, this limestone ground
lying miles from any town. At our age, to begin again!

So he can call his cattle with this grandfather's *woo-kee* cry.
I can have my solitude, a view of gray rock out the kitchen window.

He still eats without speaking. I'm as stubborn
but now can pad the pitch dark, room to room, know light switches,

kitchen drawers, shapes of speckled limestone running
north-south through the farm like a school of gray whales

forever mid-breach in the grasses
right where the glaciers left them.

Spousal Psalm in the Key of C Major

The flesh and the body
your flesh on your body
flesh of myself
out in the world
flesh through the world
an opposite arm
pining for this
and all that came before
no better, no worse
animal flesh
flesh of myself
flesh of your fingers
your unspoken tongue
how could you not?—
smell of your flesh
flesh of ourselves
without end

my flesh on my body
carne incarnate
flesh of yourself
our bodies moving
swinging a leg
in balance, in rhythm
desirous of that
to come again
come in from the world
from animal body
recalling your flesh
deeper than skin
as you recall mine—
smell of my flesh
savor the skin-covered
in and out of the world
ending not with *Amen*

but with *Ahh*.

Annus Mirabilis, Annus Horribilis at the Rock's Hard Place

All the hungry, little voices
inside the small blue eggs inside the robin.

The black bull in his winter pen
not yet turned out to service.

Thistle, blueweed, pale-leaf mullein,
wild olive in the rocks.

A small mind, quietly placed,
birds worthwhile in the bush.

The mud and twig nest
lying beside a dove hatchling,

neck askew,
now deconstructed too.

Where the pond was, weeds mown
in straight green rows, I mean that dry.

The cow's oozing tumor of an eye:
buzzards land where she has lain. That putrid.

His saying his doctor called
to say his cancer counts shot up.

The role of random given to the wolf,
how about the lamb for once?

      **

Thistle, blueweed, fat-stemmed mullein,
its coming does not mean it's here.

**

Thistle, blueweed, yellow-flowered mullein:
remedy for cough, congestion,

charm to ward off demons
before it shrivels brown.

His pallor colored with transfusion.
Cowbirds travel with the cattle,

the flock's low flight: small fat brown forward-flying
thoughts through the Queen Ann's Lace

he called *wild carrot*, thick and white as any planted crop,
thick as cells, thick as thieves: the cowbirds, cattle and the weeds,

pastures seeming peaceful from this distance.
A couple sitting on a porch:

the picture of long marriage,
seeming peaceful too.

Lowing cattle become childhood's rustled herds,
herds the hero, in the end, recovers

before big music of his riding off.
Cookie out there somewhere

cooking beans
for dipping up onto tin plates.

**

I meant the frying pan's fire, the rock's hard place,
all the feathers flocked together.

I meant swimming in the devil's deep blue,
the black dog gnawing mossy stones she gathered.

    **

Pills to sleep. Pills to smile.
Hot bitter taste of morning, cut with cream.

Neighbors' target practice, off and on,
autumn Sundays the crack and boom of calibers.

Pills to eat. Pills to not.
Quiet hangs like curtains, pause enough to think

intermission's reload is the end.
Deer drift out of thinning cover.

A killdeer circles higher
than I have ever seen a killdeer fly.

In fact, I have never seen a killdeer
do anything but its hurt-wing decoy flutter.

    **

Of course it's coming.
Pills to crap. Pills to breathe

put under the tongue.
The short lyric of a long song,

its mourning dove refrain
as always there as air.

One pill, then another: oval, round.
There is the point

of the plow, tines of the harrow,
time, though bent, the one straight line

while high in the cedar
a Ruby-Crested Kinglet hangs

upside down, one leg tangled
in a strand of twine: a harvest still-life

(when not struggling).
The razor blade duct-taped

to a found pole cuts the cord
and the Ruby-Crested Kinglet tumbles

through the cedar limbs, then flies off, trailing twine.
And here I was trying to be kind.

  **

Bones with tufted hair and sinew
dot the yard, both dogs stink of scavenge.

This is the waiting.
This is the sip and the slow breath

or last night's dream hovering over window
glass's dark reflective.

This is the scratch of small claws
scurrying inside the walls,

the time of soft light in emptying woods
as yesterday's leaves cover what had fallen.

Today hangs in the trees.
This is the time between times,

held breath to better
hear the scratching claws inside the walls.

      **

The bull's back in the bull lot
behind board fence and clicking wire.

Gray days come like gray pearls
strung around the neck.

It's dark by five.
The ground has winter bone.

This is the time of deer rut,
rifle boomings from the woods.

There are people out there
on a nation's Kill or Capture list.

      **

On the porch steps cat puke coils of gray
indeterminate flesh as bloodless

as Shylock would have wished
Antonio's to be, the ropy mess

topped by one upright
perfectly intact rodent ear

as if still listening for the cat
it failed to hear.

Swallow

Fledgling
   from summer's
first clutch, lying
   wings out, downy
but breathing
   in the barn aisle,
light as nothing
   in my palm, set down
on some mulch
   where its spine
in time
   became an S
of small white dots
   concluding in a tiny
cranium
   and diamond
double V
   of open beak.

Due to the Attraction of the Moon and Sun

Tide slides out
imperceptible

past all grasp

Dark wet sand
underlines the sea.

Pad the house
that one last time,

like chaps and saddle
chaps stiffened round,

where calf met flank

at first
as he in his—

flaccid and away.

at low tide

barefoot, a saline waft
unforgotten—just set aside

on hook and rack,
sweat-stained dark with use

in the language of the ride.

Before My Lover Was a Bird

My lover was a fish
silver-sided flash in tree-shade shallows.
My lover was not shallow
but quiet as a fish.
His mouth mouthed *oh, oh.*
He slid through blood-cold shadows.
We drank the water where he swam.
A requiem is not a psalm.

After my lover was a bird,
peach-beaked singer of shaped notes
sweetened through his white throat,
a small, seed-eating bird,
the color of the dirt
he foraged in—his beak could hurt—
after bird, my lover was spring lamb.
Every idol is the I Am.

When my lover was a lamb
before he grew into a slit-eyed ram—
tu-wit, tu-woo, one never knew.
Then he settled down as ram.
We wore his wool, soft and thick.
To the god of Abraham and Isaac,
his black tongue bleated: *Oblivion. Heretic.*

Rock the Billy Goat Out of his Gruff

Cradle the cow. Polish the spoon. Whisper
good-night to the slivered new moon.
Let go the dream words not coming back

not now, maybe never, as first they were dreamed.
Walk the dog into mute light.
Birdsong enlarges in cloud-covered ways,

as the childhood dream, in slight disguise
of fragment and phrase,
rises clear in the sway of its music:

the kick at the end of the foot;
the smack of the ball in the air;
the run and the shout and the throw;

the call at the end of the day—
your name on the tongue of the breeze,
syllables thick in the sound of the world

with the cry of the home
to come in from the game
to your place someone set at the table.

Are Sunsets More Beautiful in Winter?

My neighbor and I, we call each other.
Her house sits on a rise
across the county road from mine.
Quick. Look. Go see the sky.

She takes iPad pictures.
I often think about him:
pillowed head turned to the window,
bare forearms bruised as any sunset,

how he said, a day or two
before he died
in a high-pitched voice that was
and wasn't his:

*You'd have to be a real sick man
not to see that sky.*

On Re-reading His Hospice Journal: The Living Relic

I wrote he said:

> *Burn what's left and spread it here.*
> *That's easiest. No feeding tubes.*

Deer! sends both dogs past pointed finger,
launched on faith

in what the yoga teacher calls
the season of metal, the season of grief.

Locust leaves like fish food flakes
drift down in yellow scatter.

Flash cards of his final days make myth
of memory.

> *I don't trust me either.*

You come to
whoever calls, no question.

Sit and stay
or come too, a choice.

> *I'm not much count anymore.*
> *Come sit with me.*

The cat rubs up against the dog.
The horse rubs up against the dawn

the train rumbles through
as I relive an Old Testament

that never aged, was never new,
him four years dead tomorrow.

> *I didn't forget, just got confused*
> *on what I remember.*

And,

> *Bring a lockjaw then,*
> *because I can still overpower you women.*

Is he kidding?, asked the triage nurse.
Not sure, I said,

knowing full well he was not.
How the frayed edge of his living relic

unraveled to strike out
with his oxygen container—

twice swung from its strap—
sick as he was!—

first my shoulder, then defensive forearm.
His eyes' glittering assessment:

> *I could hurt you*

all made his dying, if not easy, easier. There is that.
The second year harder than the first.

> *I am completely out of my wits.*

How burrs like spoken words embed the dogs' coats,
solve the burdock's planted problem.

Stay meant
thorn and bramble in a bird-thick place,

chirp and warble,
the quieting screech of September.

Stay meant ignore
the neighbor's rooster's infinitum

but hear the wild birds' warble
all the down dog sit and stay.

Small Dark Mysteries

Head to tail-tip: low dark creatures scurry
across the road. Four in view, probably more in all,
hurrying toward roadside weeds.
Mink, maybe. Maybe weasel. Muskrat, even—
small, long-bodied with fur so dark and thick
I'm guessing mink. Paws tentative on asphalt.
Urgent too, not knowing, I imagine, why or where to,
just keeping to a sibling order, holding to the group.

Muskrat, mink or weasel, whatever kits are on the move
I watch what I can't name, what I have not seen before,
most likely will not see again, having lived this long
for my first view—find myself their palms-up traffic guard
until all the small dark mysteries have crossed,
the roadside leaves cease shaking and no predator
or lagging afterthought appears.

Aubade at Kitchen Window

The seeded feeder swaying peaceful for the most part,
peaceful but for the hammer-headed jays.

Who can name one scene that lacks—implied
or otherwise—its hammer-headed jays?

To wander the what-if landscape
under dark of threatened rain, swollen knuckles aching,

tide slides out the way he left:
imperceptible until it's not. *Do you have to hit every pothole?*

Never mind the scold-bird, no matter its insistence
within the thorny branches of the honey locust tree,

its cry may be mere transference of another voice you knew.
The siren's sudden wail *Not me, Not me*

some miles away and fading *Not here, Not now*
into a feet-up peace before the daily stirrings:

the dogs' deep rhythmic breathing, click of ceiling fans.
All teaspoons, it is true, but spilling in abundance.

Somewhere out there may be found the kindness of a cat,
way out beyond the birds.

Winter secrets shouted out: what's living and what's dead.
The great upheaval is beneath us, bare white given way

to prime dandelion time, the brevity of bluebells,
old adversaries of poke, wild onion picking up

where they left off as if they had never been away
which, of course, they hadn't.

Wendell Hawken lives on a grass farm in the northern Shenandoah Valley in the company of two dogs and one cat. After retiring from office work, Hawken earned her MFA in Poetry from the Warren Wilson College Program for Writers where she studied with Betty Adcock and Ellen Bryant Voigt among others. She has two full collections, *The Luck of Being* (The Backwaters Press, 2008), and *White Bird: A Sequence*, (FutureCycle Press, 2017), which was honored by the Library of Virginia with a 2018 Literary Award. A chapbook, *The Spinal Sequence,* was published by Finishing Line Press in 2013.

www.ingramcontent.com/pod-product-compliance
Lightning Source LLC
LaVergne TN
LVHW041522070426
835507LV00012B/1757